5.50

D1592817

Anglican–Orthodox Pilgrimage

edited by
Franklin Billerbeck

Conciliar Press
Ben Lomond California

Library of Congress Cataloging-in-Publication Data

Anglican–Orthodox pilgrimage / edited by Franklin Billerbeck
    p. cm.
    Includes bibliographical references
ISBN 0-9622713-5-7 : $4.50
    1. Converts, Orthodox Eastern—United States—Biography.
    2. Ex-church members—Anglican Communion—Biography.
    3. Orthodox Eastern Church—Apologetic works.
    4. Anglican Communion—Controversial literature.
I. Billerbeck, Franklin, 1960–
BX739.A1A54 1993
230'.19,dc20   93-23496
                                          CIP

TABLE OF CONTENTS

INTRODUCTION

In increasing numbers, Anglicans are coming home to Orthodox Christianity. In a recent study, Anglicans were the second largest group of converts to the Orthodox Church in America.[1] Numerous new congregations have been formed by former Anglicans in the Antiochian Orthodox Archdiocese, an archdiocese in which over half of the clergy are converts, many of them former Anglicans.

This booklet provides the stories of ten Anglican converts to Orthodoxy. They are different in age, background, and interests, and they hail from different parts of the United States. Some are clergy, some are lay. Many of them were in positions of leadership within Anglicanism before they became Orthodox. But here, they have all found peace and spiritual growth in the stability of the Faith "once delivered."

For those interested in learning more about Orthodoxy, sources for more information and a list of contact people are provided at the end of this booklet.

---

1 Sara Loft, *Converts Respond* (Syosset, New York: The Orthodox Church in America, 1984), pp. 3, 12, 16.

TWENTY MONTHS INTO ORTHODOXY

by Father William Olnhausen

Just after Easter, 1989, the Episcopal Bishop of Milwaukee, correctly perceiving my loyalty to Orthodoxy, offered me the choice of resignation or an ecclesiastical trial. The charges? "Apostasy," said he!

I think I could have survived the trial, but to what purpose?

For me, this was the sign from God that it was time to go home. I resigned as rector of Saint Boniface Church, in the Milwaukee suburb of Mequon, and renounced the ministry of the Episcopal Church. This made the front page of the *Milwaukee Journal* and even appeared in the Wisconsin news of *USA Today*, right next to the item about a crooked lobbyist in Madison!

When I left, on June 3, 1989, I knew for certain of only five people, one of whom was my wife, who wanted to become Orthodox with me. I was frightened and prepared to take secular work. I had already decided to join the Antiochian Archdiocese, under His Eminence, Metropolitan Philip. At the direction of Father Peter Gillquist (a former evangelical, author of *Becoming Orthodox*, now chairman of the Archdiocesan Department of Missions and Evangelism), we began Orthodox inquirers' classes, which attracted about thirty people.

By the end of the summer, about fifteen of us were

ready to become Orthodox—far fewer than I had hoped for, but enough to get started. On September 16, 1989, at Saints Constantine and Helen Greek Orthodox Church in Wauwatosa, Wisconsin, His Grace, Bishop Antoun chrismated us and ordained me subdeacon and then deacon. (I was an Orthodox layman for about ten minutes!) The next day, at rented facilities in Mequon, I was ordained priest, and we were on our way. Quickly, other Episcopalians and some Orthodox people joined us.

Today, twenty months later, we have a multi-ethnic congregation of twenty-five households, with Sunday attendance continually growing. Our people are giving generously, and I have been supported full-time from the beginning. The congregation is now meeting in a school basement, but we are about to purchase property, and we hope to have a building in due time. God has been good!

THE FIRST TWELVE MONTHS

My first year as an Orthodox priest was very busy. Besides the work of forming a congregation, I had to learn a new liturgical system, and also took an extensive series of correspondence courses required by the Archdiocese. I did not and still do not have words even remotely adequate to describe what has happened to me and my people. Orthodoxy is very different on the inside (far better, I hasten to add!) from the way it appears from the outside.

As an Anglo-Catholic I thought I was "catholic"; I thought I understood the Faith. But becoming Orthodox has changed my world-view, my concept of the Church, my interior life, even the very categories in which I think. I have come to see why Saint Paul withdrew and kept silent for three years after his conversion. I now understand why Orthodoxy stresses apophatic theology (the idea that we speak of God in terms of what He is *not*, because human language is incapable of expressing what He *is*): much of what I have experienced goes so far beyond words. But now, with fear and trembling and only twenty months' experience, let me try to express what little I can.

Let me say first that the Orthodox Church, seen from a human perspective, seems imperfect, no refuge from human sins or failings. Anyone who comes to Orthodoxy in order to escape problems will be disappointed. Father Alexander Schmemann, it is said, once exclaimed, "The Orthodox Church is the right Church filled with the wrong people!" He overstated his case. Indeed, I have never before experienced so much love, support, and personal warmth as I have found in the Orthodox Church. If you become Orthodox, prepare to be hugged a lot!

In truth, all Churches are filled with the "wrong people," and there are at least as many sinners in Orthodoxy as in any other group. The Orthodox Church in the USA is particularly plagued by jurisdictional divisions, ethnic xenophobia, considerable lack of missionary zeal, and a lot of nominal members. And yet . . . And yet . . . .

THE UNITY OF THE FAITH

As compared to Anglicanism, there is a very different inner "dynamic" in the Orthodox Church. The Episcopal Church contains many good, faithful people who care deeply and work hard defending the Faith. Yet the inner dynamic of the Episcopal Church obviously tends towards heresy, disunity, departure from the Faith. Despite her sinful members, including myself, the Orthodox Church tends towards orthodoxy, unity, and commitment to the Faith.

At first I disbelieved the claim that the Orthodox Church possesses "theological unanimity." It still astounds me. I have yet to meet a member of the Orthodox Church—clergy or lay—who disbelieves the Virgin Birth, the Incarnation, or the Resurrection. "Of course we're against abortion," said one of my "cradle Orthodox" parishioners; "we're Orthodox."

Many non-Orthodox assume that, as the Orthodox Church becomes more Americanized, it will necessarily take the same path into doctrinal innovation that Western denominations have followed. I have questioned many Orthodox about this—theologians, professors, deans, bishops, monks, parish priests, laypersons—and few see any sign of it. Bishop Kallistos (formerly Timothy Ware, ex-Anglican and author of *The Orthodox Church*) told me that his fear is rather that Orthodoxy, in reaction to the West, will withdraw into itself, preserving its doctrinal purity but not sharing it with others.

Orthodoxy insists that, despite the failings of her members, the Church herself is perfect. Why? Because that is how Orthodox Christians experience the Church—not as "Christ's leprous bride," as one Episcopal bishop often describes her, but as the pure and spotless Bride of Christ, as the New Testament describes her. My experience of the Church as an Orthodox Christian is utterly different from my experience of the Church as an Anglican.

I believe that the inner dynamic of Orthodoxy is simply the Holy Spirit, and that the Orthodox Church is simply the Church. I ask you: Where else today can you find the Church described by Saint Irenaeus, which believes apostolic teachings everywhere "alike, as if she had but one heart and one soul, and preaches them harmoniously, teaches them, and hands them down, as if she had but one mouth" (*Adv. Haereses*, III)?

FROM PERSONAL EXPERIENCE

I came to Orthodoxy, weary of ever-shifting doctrines and morals, seeking stability in the Faith. I have found what I sought—but even more, I have found the Kingdom of God. The fourth Sunday I celebrated the Divine Liturgy, it was as if a door opened and I stepped into heaven—and I haven't stepped out. Various members of my congregation have had similar "breakthroughs," usually at worship.

Just before becoming Orthodox in 1989, my wife returned from attending Divine Liturgy in another town, exclaiming, "I just worshipped for the first time!" Once you open yourself up to it, Orthodox worship is Spirit-filled like nothing else I have ever experienced. I have no adequate words even to begin to describe or explain its reality.

There is power in the Sacrament of Chrismation, the gift and seal of the Holy Spirit. Orthodoxy is careful never to suggest that the presence of the Holy Spirit is confined to sacraments or to the institutional Church. I knew God, His presence and His power, when I was an Anglican. Nevertheless, there has also been a new "dynamic" in *me* since I have been Orthodox—disciplining me, shaping me, sometimes accusing me in a not altogether pleasant way, urging me up from my spiritual sloth. Again, I haven't the words to express this, but I am sure that chrismation has indeed caused the Holy Spirit to move in a new way in my life.

The biggest personal change has been in my mental outlook. As an Anglo-Catholic, I had become narrow, defensive, almost perpetually depressed. I felt backed up against the wall. It seemed I was spending so much time and energy merely trying to justify my existence. I felt I was at the end of something beautiful which was dying. As an Orthodox, I feel thoroughly supported in the Faith, so that I can begin to open up and grow again.

As an Orthodox Christian in America, I believe I am at the beginning of something glorious. Though old-country ethnic Orthodoxy is naturally declining in America, the Orthodox mission to America is just beginning. I can't speak from experience for the situation in other Orthodox jurisdictions, but I see that the missionary thrust of my own Antiochian Archdiocese is organized, dynamic, exciting. In this largely English-speaking archdiocese, the majority of clergy are converts, and our number of congregations has nearly tripled in the past twenty-five years.

My wife notices the change in me especially when I come home from clergy conferences. After latter-day Episcopal clergy gatherings, it took her a week or more to cheer me up and glue me back together again, but I return from Orthodox clergy conferences happy as can be. I am enthusiastic and positive-minded about the Church. I love it.

TURNING THE CORNER

I found the transition to Orthodoxy far easier than I had anticipated. There have been difficulties, of course. One needs to approach Orthodoxy with an open mind, prepared to learn and change. Those who come hoping merely to preserve all of their old Anglican ways (of whatever sort) in a new setting are invariably unhappy. It can't be done.

Largely for that reason, we chose Byzantine Rite Orthodoxy. It seems to me to offer a fuller, richer, deeper form of worship. Byzantine Rite was hard to master, but not as hard as I had expected, and my people appear genuinely to love it. Does Byzantine Rite seem foreign and "Eastern"? No more so than the Scriptures, which were not exactly the product of the Western European mind, after all. No one has pressured us to become Greek, Russian, or Arab ethnics. We are allowed, even encouraged, to be "American ethnic" Orthodox—or, as one member of my congregation puts it, "Midwestern Orthodox"!

Occasionally one hears a horror story about an Anglican who becomes Orthodox, has a negative experience, and returns. There are such cases. But compare that with the horror of what modern Anglicanism is doing to her traditional members and their faith *daily*. There is certainly no guarantee that everyone's transition into Orthodoxy will be as easy as mine. But I tell you: whatever the cost, it is worth it. In fact, there are myriads of former Anglicans who are now happily Orthodox. I find them everywhere.

LOOKING BACK

I hesitate to speak negatively of a denomination of which I am no longer a member; Anglicanism is no longer mine to criticize. So let me put it this way: What on earth did I think I was doing in the Episcopal Church? From my present perspective, Anglicanism seems so obviously to be a liberal Protestant denomination, not the catholic Church. This is why, in the end, I had no difficulty with being "reordained." I had concluded that, as an Anglican priest, I was not part of the catholic ministry in its fullness.

Let me try to say this gently: It is surprising how narrow, limited, and ethnic (yes, ethnic!) Anglicanism appears from the outside. Culturally, the Episcopal Church is exceedingly monochrome, while the Orthodox Church is multi-ethnic, comprised of people of many national, social, and economic backgrounds—a fascinating and challenging mix which has broadened my Christian perspective immensely. Anglicanism and its problems, seen from here, seem almost quaint and old-fashioned. As we read of John Spong's latest escapades or of the struggles with twisted morality or of the female priesthood, my wife sometimes asks, "Are they still arguing about *that*?"

Do I miss Anglicanism? Of course. There has been much that is beautiful and holy in her heritage. There are many good and gracious Episcopalians. But I have rarely been tempted to look back. In every way, Orthodoxy seems richer, fuller, more complete, more *permanent*. In our congregation, we have been allowed to retain some of our Western musical tradition, but in fact we are gradually replacing much of it, for it seems a bit "thin" in the context of Orthodox worship.

In sum, I cannot imagine going back.

TO THOSE WHO REMAIN BEHIND

My chief message to my dear Anglican friends is that we're alive and well and enthusiastic about living in the Holy Orthodox Church. I wish you were here, too. I respect and admire those of you who are suffering and fighting for the Faith in the Episcopal Church. For purposes not clear to me, God may have some reason for keeping you there. Who am I to pass judgment?

But isn't it obvious that Anglicanism itself has failed? Why do you want to preserve a system that has become a hindrance to the Faith? Instead of being consumed by trying to defend yourself from a jaded, increasingly post-Christian Anglicanism, you could be working to convert people to Orthodoxy, to a Church which defends and supports her members in the Faith.

But again, beware: Do not come to Orthodoxy as the best option, as a better place to be. Come only if you see the Orthodox Church as the *one* real option. Come only if you are prepared to leave your Anglican baggage behind, prepared to learn, to change, to grow, to open yourself in all humility to the wisdom of this Church which, so different from all the others, still remains genuinely united in Apostolic Faith.

Father Olnhausen is pastor of Saint Nicholas Mission (Antiochian), Mequon, Wisconsin.

TASTE AND SEE

by Mary M. Stolzenbach

Forty years ago, a little girl raised in the Presbyterian Church, like me, could get to know the Scriptures rather well. For this I will always be grateful. Most of all I am grateful to God for giving me a persistent love and desire for Him which has followed me throughout my life.

During my college years, I spent much time studying the Bible and theology, hungering to know more about the God of my youth. I joined the Episcopal Church because its tradition fed my desire for beauty in worship. Also attractive was the Church's support for the civil rights movement, a cause I championed. Yet early on I began to see that all was not well with this Church of beauty and conviction. All too often, I observed the sincere efforts to bring Christian belief into the events of the day degenerating into frustration, hatred for one's enemies, and an unspiritual way of life.

The preaching, while eloquent, became subtly infected with destructive biblical criticism and modernist theology. I had studied enough of the same books to recognize what the carefully qualified statements and evasions of the preachers meant. Somehow the heart had been cut out of these men's faith. I grew more and more discouraged, receiving no sustenance or leadership from my Church. I was married by this time, and my husband gave me much love and support. He too, however, was spiritually searching.

When I reached the point of desperation, God graciously intervened to give me, through the charismatic movement, an experience of Himself that convinced me of His reality and His love. Through this experience we became involved in fellowship with many dedicated evangelical and fundamentalist believers.

These enthusiastic Christians loved God, but I soon discovered that they, too, had a sadly incomplete understanding of Him. They seemed quite willing to believe God *wanted* to send most of the human race to hell, including many who professed the Christian Faith. They even knew just who was on His list! When I spoke of my deep lifelong desire to serve God and obey His commands, they shook their heads and warned of "vain works." The evangelical Protestant version of Church history was shallow and incomplete, and they completely sidelined the sacraments and the saints.

For these and other reasons, we did not consider joining these brethren, but turned our hopes and prayers back to renewing our own Episcopal Church. The years were passing, though, and the lack of faith had by now begun to give birth to open false teaching and immoral behavior. These went undisciplined by the men at the top, some of whom were in fact leaders in the false teaching.

By 1986, we had begun to attend from time to time an Orthodox Church near our home. I was immediately drawn to the beauty of the worship, but many questions persisted in my mind. Orthodoxy is new to most of us Americans, and it takes time to see in what way, as the priest put it, "the Church does what Jesus does. We are the Church of the biblical world."

My husband had now reached a position of service and influence as a layman in our Episcopal parish. He had more to give up than I. As we looked further into Orthodoxy we saw, as well as the beauty and splendor, the weakness, scandals, and divisions that must surely grieve Christ so much, and we were deeply distressed. I thank God that we were not given a falsely rosy picture. As Father Thomas Hopko wrote to us, "the true Church—which realizes itself in sacramental worship in all of its splendor and beauty and truth—is itself plagued by the sins of its earthly members. It is always in the midst of *internal* conflict."

I waited in anxiety, because I knew my husband and I belonged together and yet I did not see how I could go on as an Episcopalian. I was sick of false teaching, and because of my faith in the Holy Spirit, I knew that the Church Christ founded had to have been around from the beginning. There were really only two candidates for *that* position.

We had, in fact, looked into the Roman Catholic Church, but we did not see how we could unite in faith with all that she taught, and she no longer even seemed sure of her faith. "Lord, to whom shall we go?" was often in my mind. So we prayed, and waited, as Father Hopko advised. As I prayed and attended Divine Liturgy, the teaching of Orthodoxy began to soak into my heart and mind.

"For He is good, and loves mankind" was the Orthodox answer to my fundamentalist friends. "Bow your heads to the Lord!" was her answer to the revolutionaries in the Episcopal Church and elsewhere who were remaking God and Christ into the images *they* preferred. To be called "the servant of God" was the answer to my longings from childhood.

It seemed almost miraculous to me when one dark autumn evening in 1988, my husband said to the priest, Father Paul, "We've come to your house tonight to ask you to receive us into the Orthodox Church as soon as possible."

Every moment of the ceremony was beautiful and right. After we made our confession of faith, Father Paul told us to hold the ends of his stole as he led us forward for absolution and blessing before the book of the Gospel which represents Christ in our midst. Later, we stood and listened to that Gospel.

Father Paul read of the woman who had touched Jesus' robe and been healed, and was then called forward to acknowledge her faith. And I saw how, in a mystery, we had just done the same thing. "The Church does what Jesus does."

When at last we went forward to receive Communion for the first time in the Holy Orthodox Catholic Church, I knew that my lifelong search for the fullness of God had led me to this place of beauty and ageless serenity, of Spirit and truth. In my joyous heart were the words of the psalmist: "Taste and see how good the Lord is; happy the one who takes refuge in Him."

Mary and Conrad Stolzenbach attend Holy Trinity Church (OCA) in Reston, Virginia.

A LETTER: LEAVING ANGLICANISM AND ENTERING ORTHODOXY

This letter was sent by Henry and Leaella Shirley and William Draper to their Christian friends on the occasion of their joining the Orthodox Church. Formerly members of Saint James Episcopal Church, Milwaukee, they now belong to Saints Cyril and Methodius Orthodox Church (OCA) in Milwaukee.

June 5, 1988
Sunday of All Saints/Pentecost II

Dear Brothers and Sisters in Christ:

As some of you know, we have decided to leave Anglicanism (and its American province, the Protestant Episcopal Church) and to be received by chrismation into Orthodoxy—more specifically the Orthodox Church in America (formerly a part of the Russian Orthodox Church). This action is surrounded with much grief at leaving, yet filled with the deep joy of finally "going home." After so many years as Anglicans, we feel obliged to explain our reasons—both to our friends and to those in positions of pastoral oversight and responsibility within Anglicanism. Below are two statements on the essentially separate issues of why we feel compelled to leave and why we have chosen the Orthodox Church.

ON LEAVING ANGLICANISM

It does not occur to us to be anything other than catholics. We became Episcopalians because we were taught and believed that the Anglican communion was a legitimate expression of the catholicism of English-speaking people. Our confirmations or reception were a statement that we believed the Episcopal Church to be part of the One, Holy, Catholic, and Apostolic Church. But we can no longer make that affirmation except by the widest exercise of scholastic reasoning and mental gymnastics.

We have come to believe that by its open repudiation of the faith and practice of the undivided Church—established by Christ, recorded in Scripture, proclaimed by the Apostles, and taught by the Fathers and seven Ecumenical Councils—the Episcopal Church has forfeited any claim it may have once had to be part of or in doctrinal continuity with that Church. Some provinces of the Anglican communion have taken similar actions, and still others by their silence and lack of clear statement to the contrary (they remain in communion with PECUSA), have given tacit consent.

We also believe that a rereading of the documents surrounding the English reformation and the writings of the seventeenth-century Anglican divines indicates that the defects of which we now see the end results were inherent from the beginning. There was bound to be trouble in churches where the highest doctrinal authority is the King in Parliament, or the whims of a mere provincial synod also known as the General Convention, and not the Scriptures, Creeds, and decrees of the Ecumenical Councils as guarded by the whole people of God, and as taught and proclaimed by bishops in succession to and continuity with the Apostolic Church.

It is with reluctance that we write these things. It is with genuine regret that we make these statements. We have loved the Anglican ethos, liturgy, and piety in varying forms—from the witness of those who worshipped, worked, and prayed for the reunion of the Anglican Churches with the Holy See of Rome, to the real evangelical testimony of Anglo-Catholicism, even in its autumn ("Catholic worship—Gospel preaching"), to the sometimes quixotic yet always faithful dreams of those who hoped to someday see the Rite of Sarum in common usage. This is not easy for us.

What follows is a list of events which have led us to take this step, and which brought us (individually, and before we considered Orthodoxy) to know in our hearts that we had to leave, and to give that leaving to God as an offering, asking Him to show us the direction we should go, even if it meant, as Blessed John Henry Newman wrote in 1833, being "far from home."

1) The Episcopal Church, along with other provinces of the Anglican communion, purports to have "ordained" women to the priesthood. It claims to have the authority to consecrate women as bishops. This is so radical a departure from the unbroken practice of the Church as to call into question not only the validity of such ordinations, but also whether Anglicanism is part of the Church

Catholic or simply another form of denominational Protestantism. We fear the latter. The simple fact is that there is no warrant (scriptural or otherwise) for the ordination of women to episcopal or presbyterial office. Christianity knows nothing of priestesses.

2) The Episcopal Church has demonstrated abject moral cowardice in its failure to speak the truth in the face of the murder of over twenty million unborn American children. To take the position that although human life is sacred from its inception, the decision to end that life is the sole affair of the mother in consultation with her priest strikes us as ethical "new-speak."

3) Although the Episcopal Bishop of Milwaukee and a national commission appointed by the Presiding Bishop have tried to uphold the Church's traditional teaching regarding human sexuality, the Bishop of Newark and others continue to openly sanction, and urge the Church to bless, sexual relations outside of heterosexual marriage. Bishops in the Episcopal Church have ordained openly practicing homosexuals to the priesthood. Organizations advocating licit sexual congress outside of marriage meet and operate out of our cathedral churches. Who has called these bishops and priests to account? No one seems concerned enough about the open scandal of Bishop Spong to secure enough clergy and laymen to bring a presentment against him. What witness does the Episcopal Church give to the world, when it tolerates almost any moral evil or eccentricity for the sake of supposed "unity"?

4) Anglican liturgy and hymnody have been revised and debased solely for the sake of "inclusiveness." Deliberate mistranslations of Scripture have been made (especially in the Psalter) so as to eliminate references to "maleness" which offend feminists. The Standing Liturgical Commission has proposed alternative texts for the Eucharist and Daily Offices (actually used in all but one seminary of the church) which are blatantly heretical in intent and run contrary to the clear biblical standard which has always been a touchstone for the Anglican rites.

The earliest Christian proclamation was "Jesus Christ is Lord." The incarnate Son of God taught us to call the first Person of the Holy Trinity "Father." The words "lord" and "father" apparently bother some who are on the cutting edge of modern theological speculation. They also bother those whose agenda for the Church is clearly secular and political. The preface to the proposed alternative rites expresses the hope that Episcopalians may one day feel comfortable referring to God as "mother." As Kallistos Ware has written, "A mother goddess is not the Lord of the Christian Church." Sadly, the Church is prepared to use and publish heretical rites rather than suggest that the problem may be with those who cannot deal with the Christian revelation.

5) The Church of England, with the Archbishop of Canterbury presiding, has consecrated as Bishop of Durham a man who denies the bodily resurrection of Our Lord Jesus Christ. Bishop Jenkins has expressed the opinion that the Resurrection consists primarily in the apostles' experience of a continuing relationship with

Jesus after the crucifixion.

Twenty years ago Bishop James Pike denied the doctrine of the Trinity. No one cared enough about either the doctrine or Bishop Pike to bring a presentment for heresy against him. (More correctly, there were not enough bishops to bring such a presentment to the point of ecclesiastical trial.) Apparently, Anglicanism cares more for "comprehensiveness" than it does for the basic doctrines of the faith.

6) The Episcopal Church has allowed and encouraged ministers who have not been ordained by bishops in the apostolic succession to officiate in priestly or diaconal capacity. The desire for unity with Protestant Christians has led to yet another instance of the dilution of apostolic faith and practice in the quest for a generally acceptable ecclesiastical minimalism.

When the Archbishop of Canterbury preached at the installation of the new presiding bishop of the Evangelical Lutheran Church in America, it could have been a genuine instance of the future healing of division for which we all pray. But when he received communion at the same service, it was a statement that the apostolic faith which he is sworn to defend is capable of compromise. Anglicanism does no service to the wider Christian community or to itself by its continued and repeated indications that, while it officially stands for catholic faith and practice, it enforces neither.

7) Women's ordination, compromise on abortion, and sexual morality, worship geared to the "spirit of the age,"

bishops who preach heresy, failure to uphold the catholic and apostolic order of ministry—all are symptoms. The underlying issue is whether or not Christianity is revealed. The essential Faith of the Church is found in the Scriptures and Creeds. Either we take the events of our salvation seriously and with implications for how we worship, believe, and live our lives in the world, or we do not. Either we believe in the Holy Trinity, the Incarnation and Virgin Birth, the Resurrection, the Church as established by Christ and the continued indwelling of the Holy Spirit in the Church, or we do not. The question is not whether these things make sense in the light of modern psychology, anthropology, or political theory, but whether or not they are the Truth.

In its last Pastoral Letter to the Church, the House of Bishops has given an answer to the questions above. The bishops, sworn at their consecrations to "guard the faith, unity and discipline of the Church" (BCP, p. 518), now rejoice that the Episcopal Church is "willing to lay aside all claims to the possession of infallible formulations of truth." If the Holy Scriptures and Creeds, as guarded, proclaimed, and interpreted by the Fathers and Councils, are not "infallible formulations of truth," then we may as well close the doors of our churches, because we will have nothing to give the world except nice stories and empty ritual.

There is another alternative, which we have chosen—and that is to leave.

It should be clear that our reasons for leaving the Episcopal Church are in no sense parochial. Our going has nothing to do with Saint James' parish, and certainly bears no relation to the election of the new rector. One of us served on the search committee that unanimously recommended Father Hillman's call to the Vestry. We love Saint James' and its people—it has been our home, and its people have been our family. The priest and people of Saint James' will continue to be in our prayers.

It remains only to say "thank you" to the bishops, priests, deacons, laymen, and parishes that have nourished us spiritually and in so many other ways for a collective total of nearly 60 years. If we were to list them all individually, that list might be longer than these statements.

And we must say "thank you" to the Anglican Church herself. Her liturgy, piety, and disciplines have in a very real sense prepared us for Orthodoxy. The Anglican Benedictine, Dom Gregory Dix, wrote (referring to the Church of England), "A man could and should love her . . . even if he must leave her now." We do leave loving her. And we leave mourning her. We leave grateful for that vision of the Church which she gave us—the Church as the Bride and Body of Christ, offering His worship of the Father in the beauty of holiness, and calling ordinary men and women to true sanctity. It was truly a vision glorious.

WHY ORTHODOXY?

This part of the statement is difficult to write because the decision to become Orthodox was not arrived at by any sort of careful, rational thinking and examination. It was, in fact, not really arrived at or decided by us, at all. It was rather something that happened to us. We believe that Orthodoxy is true and is logically and rationally defensible, but we came to it not by logic, but by experience, and, we believe, by the working of the Holy Spirit in our hearts. We did not decide—we simply realized one day that the decision had already been made. So what follows is not a rational explanation of the decision, but rather an attempt at a description of what happened to us, and of what we have found in Orthodoxy.

Above all else, it has been the experience of Orthodox worship that has brought us to Orthodoxy. The initial opportunity came as part of a weekend workshop sponsored by the Anglican/Orthodox Pilgrimage and held at Saints Cyril and Methodius Orthodox Church (a parish of the Orthodox Church in America) in Milwaukee. After that weekend, we continued to attend Saint Cyril's—for some Sunday Liturgies and for weekday Vespers and Matins—and we were privileged to attend almost all of the services for Holy Week and Pascha (Easter).

When the pagan Prince Vladimir of Kiev sent emissaries to investigate the Christian faith in 988, they examined various groups of Christians. After attending the Orthodox Liturgy in Constantinople, they reported to the prince, "We knew not whether we were in heaven or on earth, for surely there is no such splendor or beauty anywhere on earth. We cannot describe it to you: only this we know, that God dwells there among men, and that their service surpasses the worship of all other places. For we cannot forget that beauty."

Anglicanism (and particularly that special brand of Anglicanism known as Anglo-Catholicism) gave us a glorious vision of the fullness of Catholic faith and worship and life. We have come to believe that Orthodoxy in fact possesses that fullness we first glimpsed in Anglo-Catholicism.

In Orthodoxy we have found the faith of the undivided Church—the doctrine of the apostles, the authority of Scripture, the teaching of the seven Ecumenical Councils, and a living tradition guarding the faith. We have found the fullness of the faith, undiminished, undiluted, shining forth from the texts and actions of the Liturgy. The Blessed Trinity is no mere confusing embarrassment, mentioned one Sunday a year, but a living reality, taught in every service, in every prayer. The Mother of God is neither ignored nor enthroned in isolated splendor, but is a vital and integral part of our worship as the chief of the saints, highest of the human family of God, and given honor always because she it is who "gave birth to God the Word." The icons of the saints are censed during each service at the same time the faithful are censed because they and we are all icons of God, created in God's image. The saints are not optional "add-ons" in brackets, to be added or left out according to our personal preferences. They are a part, along with us, of the Body of Christ, the Church.

We are reminded again and again in the course of every service of how much God loves us: "He loves mankind" is a constant refrain. Over and over again in every service we are reminded of the chief events of the faith: Adam and Eve, the Fall, the Incarnation, the saving death of Christ on the "precious and life-giving Cross," and, above all, of the Resurrection in which Jesus "trampled down death by death" and saved us.

We have found rest—from the legalism and minimalism of Western Christianity and from the constant need to defend the faith from attack from within the Church as well as from outside it. We have found spiritual nourishment and growth and an eagerness to share the Gospel such as we had not felt for years.

When talking with Anglicans, we have never heard real objections raised to the truth of Orthodox beliefs. No one says, "But Orthodoxy is wrong about . . ." The objections are all on the practical level, and we know them well, for we have many times raised the same objections: "But Orthodoxy is so ethnic . . . I'm a Western Catholic . . . but I love the Western liturgy."

If the Orthodox faith is true, then whether or not it is ethnic does not finally matter—we have to follow the truth wherever it is. But though Orthodoxy (especially in this country) has been predominantly ethnic in character, it is not necessarily in and of itself particularly Russian or Greek or Serbian. The Orthodox Faith of Saint Patrick, Saint David, and our other Celtic forebears is as much ours as it is the proper possession of Russians or Greeks. As for being Westerners, there are probably none who love the western rite in its glory more than the three of us. And we will miss it. But glorious as the western rite is, what we have found in Orthodox worship is even richer and fuller.

In all this, besides gratitude to God, we owe a special debt of thanks to the pastor and people of Saints Cyril and Methodius Orthodox Church. We have been privileged to experience the fullness of Orthodox worship in our own language in a way that is unfortunately still rare in Orthodox Churches in this country. (Daily services are not common in many parishes.) We have been nourished by powerful and challenging preaching which is truly evangelical. And we have been warmly welcomed and loved and included, from the very beginning. The sign outside the church says (as many church signs do), "You Are Welcome Here." But the priest and people of Saint Cyril's have made the message of that sign a reality for us.

So, as Philip said to Nathanael, we say to our friends, "Come and see."

William H. Draper
Henry B. Shirley
Leaella J. Shirley

FROM KANSAS TO CONSTANTINOPLE

by Dr. Kent and Dena Berquist

My wife and I both grew up in small Midwestern towns. We were both raised in the Methodist Church and reached the "age of accountability" in the late 60s and early 70s.

Liberal theology had taken its toll on the Methodist Church. Consequently, our religious education was premised on ethical relativism and a distrust of Tradition. Nevertheless, the lack of historic witness, sacrament, and liturgy were not enough to keep God out. Somehow, deep down in our inner beings, seeds were planted and we began to realize that men and women were created as worshipping beings and that to fulfill our destiny, we must worship, literally bend the knee, before our Creator.

Within the first several weeks of college, members of a nondenominational, fundamentalist campus group confronted both Dena and me with the news that we were sinners in need of redemption. When confronted with this good news of salvation, we had to admit that we were in need of it and we gave our lives to Christ.

Our quest in this campus group was to practice what we called "primitive" Christianity. In retrospect we realize that there was not much correspondence between this group and the early historic Church. We simply practiced

Christianity as well as we could sort it out within an evangelical framework.

Two very important things happened during these formative years. First, the group was transformed into a Church, complete with people who approximated the roles of presbyters and bishops. Along with this came a very primitive eucharistic understanding and practice. Perhaps more important was a college friend from the same group, who introduced us to early Church history. Twenty years before our chrismations into the Orthodox Church, God in His economy was slowly setting the stage for a remarkable turning, a *metanoia*, in our understanding of Christian faith and practice.

The rigors of premedical studies slowly cooled my fervor for this brand of "primitive" Christianity. I saw the group as faltering on issues of Church order, theology, and practice. Eventually, my entrance into medical school gave us the reason we needed to leave. We spent several years dealing with our reservations and sorting out where to go next. During college we had occasionally stolen away to a Lutheran Church, drawn by its liturgy. We were attracted to liturgical worship but had not found our home.

About this time, through a providential illness, our Church historian friend found himself stranded for a year in the same city where I was training. In his absence, he had discovered the Episcopal Church and in turn, introduced us to it. For me it was love at first sight— processions, incense, vestments, crosses, genuflection, the sign of the cross, even occasional hints at Mary. Dena, on the other hand, almost had a seizure at the first sight of a processional cross. She finally agreed to give it a try based on the historical evidence that this was a reasonable expression of the ancient Church in our time.

We soon became aware of the numerous doctrinal battles raging in the Episcopal Church. The diversity of issues was initially bewildering as we tried to address each one on its particular merits. Through the guidance of a very wise priest, we realized the same objections we had concerning our campus church, which had its inception in the early 1970s, were equally valid when applied to the Episcopal (Anglican) Church, founded in the early sixteenth century. Namely, the Church was cut off from its ancient, apostolic roots. Church had become "religion a la carte"; one simply walked down the cafeteria line of life and picked from the religion section whatever seemed appealing.

It goes without saying that this kind of diet leads to serious—even terminal—spiritual illness. Eventually we found a safe haven in an Episcopal Church where a small flame of orthodox expression was kept alive. We matured within this haven and drank deeply from the Anglican well, but always with the uneasy feeling that the reservoir of Western Christendom was about to run dry.

Ten years after our historian friend had placed all of his books on Orthodoxy on loan in our library, I chanced upon Bishop Kallistos Ware's book, *The Orthodox Church*. I read with great amazement, and realized immediately that if what the author stated was true, our search had at last ended, at least intellectually. Here, clearly, was the ancient Christian Faith.

Our priest during those last few years within the Episcopal Church had an interest in Orthodoxy and informed us that Orthodoxy was alive and well in Wichita, Kansas, a mere ninety minutes from our home. Saint George Cathedral had recently been completed.

The first time my wife and I espied Saint George from several blocks off, we looked at each other and silently nodded with the solid assurance that our travels were over and that we had finally arrived home. If we had not been afraid of making a spectacle of ourselves, I'm sure we would have gotten out of the car and kissed the very ground upon which it was built.

Our first experience of Orthodox worship confirmed to us that we had found the Church of the Ages, the One, Holy, Catholic, and Apostolic Church. This service filled us with a sense of catholicity, of universality, of the whole of the Kingdom worshipping and offering thanks. A year later we were chrismated into the Orthodox Faith at Saint Mary Orthodox Church in Wichita.

It had been a year of struggle and great sadness, for we left much that was beautiful, godly, and true. We consider ourselves evangelists and are now working as we may to spread the news that while much of our culture is solidly post-Christian, and many Churches have resorted to self-mutilation in their efforts to make themselves palatable to the modern mind, the Faith of the Apostles does remain with us in Orthodoxy. The Orthodox Church is poised for the second Reformation, when believers of true faith will reform into One, Holy, Catholic, and Apostolic Church.

May God hasten that glorious day!

The Berquists attend Saint Mary's Orthodox Church (Antiochian) in Wichita, Kansas.

FINDING A HOME IN THE EASTERN RITE

by Father David Mustian

To be honest, I am not the kind of person one would expect to be "at home" in Eastern Rite Orthodoxy.

I was an Episcopal priest for ten years. Like many Anglicans, I joined the Episcopal Church as part of a journey—moving from a nonliturgical Church background, in search of the historic Church and a sacramental life. I thought my ecclesiastical search had ended when I was confirmed in a rather "High Church" Episcopal parish and diocese. I loved the silence in the Episcopal Church, the kneeling, the reverence, the "beauty of holiness," the stained glass, the splendor of Anglican chant and majestic hymns accompanied by a fine organ. It was a good place to be in 1975.

In the fall of 1975 I entered seminary at Yale Divinity School. In 1976, the ordination of women was approved, and we also were visited by "gay rights" Episcopalians who spoke of their "gains" and hopes of success at future General Conventions. All of this troubled me inwardly, but I honored my commitment to the Episcopal Church and was ordained in 1979. I had no intention of leaving.

THE RISING TIDE

As an Episcopal priest, I served in two communities. One was a small mission on the eastern plains of Colorado.

The church grew, but never fully resolved the question of ecclesiastical identity—a question I later saw as the plague of the Episcopal Church. In 1983, I was called to be assistant, and later rector, at a large parish near the University of Colorado. There were some good years in this parish, but conflict over churchmanship and the theological direction of the Church filled the final years. We tried to be "all things to all men" in a typical Anglican manner, using a variety of worship styles in separate services.

As the larger national Church began to move further away from ancient Christianity, I saw the results locally. We were trying to be an island of "Anglican orthodoxy" in the sea of a larger apostasy. Is "apostasy" too strong a word to use when credal beliefs such as the Virgin Birth and the bodily Resurrection and Ascension of our Lord are denied by some bishops without censure? Morals were also under attack. I remember a man arguing with me that his daughter should have an abortion, showing me a newspaper clipping in which an Episcopal bishop had called abortion "a moral choice."

I went to the Synod meeting in Fort Worth in 1991, hoping it would turn back the tide of apostasy. Soon it became apparent, however, that this Synod meeting would not and could not lead to an answer of any practical nature. If the Synod stayed in the Episcopal Church, it had no choice but to continue accommodating and compromising while its influence and numbers dwindled. If the Synod left the Episcopal Church, it would simply become another one of the many American denominations not in communion with anyone, neither with Canterbury nor with any of the historic patriarchates of ancient Christianity. Was the whole Anglican system of "comprehensiveness" and modern pluralism fatally flawed? I began to see that it was.

LOOKING FOR OPTIONS

In this confusion and pain, I remembered some of my seminary studies, in which I had first learned of Orthodoxy. My professor of liturgy and sacraments had taught us about Byzantine liturgy, and we had read the works of Father Alexander Schmemann. The chaplain at Yale University had literally filled the Episcopal chapel with icons, and he offered a type of daily evening Byzantine/Anglican liturgy.

I had heard of the recent movement of a group of evangelicals into Orthodoxy. I wondered if there might be a place for others sharing these convictions. Could we start an Orthodox mission? A significant part of me didn't want to be Episcopalian anymore. I didn't want to spend so much time arguing about the Faith in a losing situation, each year watching things get worse. I wanted a place where I could send my children to camp and not fear what they might be taught.

I longed for a place where the Faith was orthodox, where it did not change, where my children's children would learn the same Faith I had learned. I wanted a place where I could worship in an ancient, sacramental, liturgical manner, and where heartfelt prayer and spirituality were welcomed and encouraged. This is why I had fought my losing battle for renewal in the Episcopal Church. So I contacted Father Peter Gillquist of the Antiochian Evangelical Orthodox Mission. From that point on, the

Orthodox Church became a viable option for me. My sights were now firmly set on the Orthodox Faith.

Late in 1991, after a period of several months of study, prayer, and dialogue with Orthodox priests, I announced my resignation as rector and renounced ministry in the Episcopal Church. In January of 1992, I was chrismated and ordained as a priest in the Orthodox Church, and we began our new mission outside Boulder, Colorado. A small group of seventeen households—former Episcopalians from our previous Church—made up the initial mission.

The Lord has been with us from the beginning of this endeavor, and guided our steps wonderfully. In less than two years, our mission has more than doubled its original seventeen households. We have chrismated people from other backgrounds, ranging from Baptist to Roman Catholic. We have a newly Orthodox family from Kansas who drive four hours to be with us at least once a month. We also have been blessed with some long-time Orthodox members, such as a family who moved to our area from Saint Nicholas Cathedral in Brooklyn. We now are looking for a permanent building or land to build on.

I can honestly say I have no regrets about my decision to become Orthodox. Every passing year and each new experience confirms the rightness of that decision, and the veracity of the Orthodox Church. Fellow priests, laity, and hierarchs have been wonderful to me throughout this time, and I am extremely grateful for their help. I have indeed found the peace and stability I sought as an Episcopal priest, and I am having the best years of my life, performing the Church ministry that I had sensed a calling to do since I was a boy.

ORTHODOXY EAST OR WEST?

Looking back, one of the hardest decisions I made in this journey to Orthodoxy was not whether to become Orthodox or not, but whether to follow the Eastern or Western Rite. I am glad that my Archdiocese allows for the Western Rite. Both Rites are open to those coming to Orthodoxy from Western backgrounds, and both options are viable and worthy of careful consideration. In my particular case, God led me toward the Eastern Rite. I have been fulfilled and gratified with the results of that decision, as have the people of Saint Luke Mission. The Eastern Rite has been good for us.

Initially, I had all the typical concerns about being Eastern Rite Orthodox. I was sensitive to the length of the service, the additional services (such as Saturday Vespers), and what seemed to be excessive repetition of prayers and litanies. I also considered the ceremonial practices of veneration by kissing icons and crosses, standing instead of kneeling during Communion, and receiving the Sacrament by spoon. How would this be received by the people of our parish? Lastly, I thought of the loss of the familiar words of the Episcopal liturgy and the traditional hymns or songs, compared with the unfamiliar Byzantine tones and hymns. Was this too much change?

On the other hand, it was obvious that we were ready for a change. We knew something was very wrong in what we were coming from, and this realization gave us an openness to learn and try new things. We were joining the Orthodox Church, and it seemed logical that there would be some new ways of worship. With time, patience, and the grace of the Holy Spirit, those new things would soon become part of our very heart and soul. Indeed, that has proven to be the case.

The old Anglican value of "liturgical uniformity" also struck me as important (the *Book of Common Prayer* used to be the main thing that held Anglicans together). I wanted to be able to worship at other Orthodox Churches and feel at home in the Liturgy. I wanted our people to travel to other cities and feel at home in the Orthodox churches, which would usually be Eastern Rite.

I also found reassurance regarding my initial concerns by visiting Saint Athanasius Church in Santa Barbara, California. Here was an Eastern Rite parish, but one which obviously stressed strong congregational singing. Some of the hymn tunes were familiar. I even heard a musical instrument. My wife, who had as many concerns as I had, wept as we sang the beautiful Eastern Rite Trisagion Hymn ("Holy God, Holy Mighty, Holy Immortal One, have mercy on us"). I knew we were home. Later, Father Peter asked me, "Do you think this could play in Peoria?" I said, "Yes, I believe it could play in Peoria—and in Boulder, Colorado, too."

We were able to move gradually into the Eastern Rite, because of the pastoral wisdom and generosity of our Metropolitan Philip. Today we are much more Byzantine than when we began, but the transition has moved at a natural and comfortable pace. We also feel a degree of excitement about trying to find a musical expression of the Eastern Rite that will seem fitting to the American culture. Once again, the Orthodox Faith offers a fullness and breadth of expression which is truly encouraging and heartwarming.

I have often heard from our parishioners how glad they are that we chose this particular path, and how they feel comfortable visiting other Orthodox churches. Many have said how much they appreciate the richness of the worship—worship which is filled with symbolism, alive with icons, full of pure praise and adoration of the Holy Trinity. One of the beautifully expressive prayers I have come to love in the Eastern Rite Liturgy occurs just before the "Holy, Holy, Holy." Here the priest says, "Though there stand before You thousands of archangels and myriads of angels, cherubim and seraphim, six-winged, many-eyed, soaring high on their wings, singing, proclaiming, shouting the hymn of victory . . ."

The richness of this Liturgy is also exemplified to me in the majestic Great Entrance. It involves the Cherubic Hymn ("Let us who mystically represent the cherubim..."), with the full censing of the church, Gifts, icons, and people, and the solemn prayers of remembrance in the procession. We are drawn to heaven, and we are reminded of the offering of ourselves to God and the journey of our Lord to His crucifixion and burial.

Some who were previously low churchmen in the Episcopal Church are now participating fully in the acts of veneration, singing or chanting, and other uniquely Eastern aspects of liturgy. A few others are still growing into some of these practices.

In my observation, the Eastern Rite Liturgy, with its use of repetition, brings with it a very great depth of wisdom concerning human nature. It takes us earthbound mortals a bit of time to "lay aside all earthly cares" and enter into the Kingdom of God. Our worship is a manifestation of and preparation for heavenly worship. Repetition really *helps* here. How can we look forward to worship forever in heaven, if we have trouble with a few hours once a week now?

We have found the Byzantine hymns to be wonderfully rich in biblical allusions. They really teach the Faith. They can be simple and direct, and not hard to learn. Also, it has been good to discover that our music *can* work without having an instrument for accompaniment. Parents tell me of their little children singing some of the songs of the Liturgy at home.

AT HOME IN THE ORTHODOX CHURCH

In a Bible study we had in the Episcopal Church, I used to encourage students to "think Hebrew." Since the Bible is an "Eastern book" this advice is a helpful aid in entering into the mind and world-view of the biblical writers. It was not easy, but it made the Bible come alive. Something similar is going on with the Eastern Liturgy. It manifests a world-view different from that of our present Western culture, but I believe it reflects the world-view of the Bible in doing this.

I would be less than honest if I didn't mention that it has taken much time and learning to get to where we are today. We have spent a great deal of energy producing service booklets with the music included, which has led to good congregational participation. Whatever the commitment of time and energy involved, the transition has been worth all the effort.

Indeed, we are at home in the Orthodox Church *and* in

its Eastern Rite. And I thank God for leading us to this unchanging Church!

Father David Mustian is pastor of Saint Luke Orthodox Mission in Boulder, Colorado.

EXCESS BAGGAGE
by Father John M. Reeves

I suppose seminary is not meant to be an *easy* experience for any student—emotionally, or in any other way. Yet, for me and for my wife, beginning Episcopal seminary in the early 1970s was especially foreboding. It foreshadowed much further pain in our lives—a pain which would follow us through my ordination to the priesthood, and on into life in the parishes of the Episcopal Church.

Although I entered seminary before the ordination of women became a reality for Anglicans in the United States, the die was already cast. The authority of Scripture had long since been undermined through higher criticism (even though one was required to acknowledge the Scriptures as "the Word of God" at ordination). The Creeds were accepted, but only as "symbolic" outlines of the Christian myth in an historically conditioned fashion.

The only thing beyond attack on the seminary campus during those years seemed to be the latest opinion of the ranking professors. These higher critics were *beyond* criticism. Anyone who questioned their culturally conditioned pronouncements was considered excessively rigid—unable to cope with the ambiguity of the existential situation. Of course no student desiring to advance his career in the Church would ever want to be labeled "rigid" when it came to doctrine, morals, or revelation. So most students *rigidly* avoided any such appearance.

The remaining few were destined for the instant

pigeonhole, the label stigmatizing those who challenged the *status quo*, especially those who would have preferred the *status quo ante* (the way things used to be). In such an environment there was little approaching the stability, spiritual or intellectual, needed for honest discussion of the issues, of which women's ordination was but one.

SURVIVAL OF THE FICKLEST

In my seminary the senior year included a long and open-ended seminar. In this seminar we sat on hard wooden chairs arranged in a circle, discussing the ambiguity of our existential situation. We examined different *models* of ethics, since moral theology was not taught. As with Scripture and theology classes, we were led to explore how we felt and how we could deal with issues. The previous two years had already undermined any objective, authoritative foundation for faith. By now, our *feelings* were about all we had left.

This evolutionary approach to the Faith meant that doctrine was taught neither systematically nor dogmatically, but historically. Revelation and its meaning and interpretation were but products of history and culture. The ramifications were, of course, nothing short of tragic.

The ethics professor, for example, pondered whether the biblical commandment against adultery was still valid. His argument was threefold: (1) God, of course, had not revealed any of the Ten Commandments anyway. They were of human, not divine, inspiration. (2) The prohibition against adultery had been given to provide an agrarian society with the means to determine paternity and guard inheritance rights. (3) Modern contraception has now rendered the latter point null and void.

Or take the issue of the ordination of women. Here was the ultimate symbol of rejection of authority, both of Holy Scripture and the lived tradition of Christendom. Here also was a rejection of the Incarnation of Christ Himself. Yet one professor crassly stated: "Christ's masculinity was merely an historical accident." Another had said that Christ did not realize that he was the Messiah until he was thirty years old. Another discounted any union of the two wills in the Person of Christ; hence there could be no divine authority ascribed to Christ's selection of male apostles.

A final example: The theology professor at seminary debated with the liturgics professor over, of all things, the *filioque* clause which the Roman Catholics had inserted into the Nicene Creed. The theology professor insisted that, with or without the insertion, the Creed meant the same thing. The Holy Spirit really did proceed from the Father and the Son, no matter how one viewed it.

The liturgiologist countered that the deletion of the *filioque* was *historically* proper and facilitated dialogue with the Orthodox. Never once did either mention the eternal procession of the Spirit, or discuss the implications of John 15:26. (Of course, why should they bother, since according to the New Testament higher critics, these words probably had not been uttered by the historical Christ anyway?)

Fyodor Dostoevsky, speaking through his character, Ivan Karamazov, had it right: When there is no God, all is permitted. To my mind, such ethical posturings and theological speculations were not far from practical atheism, when seen in the light of the unchanging Tradition of historic Christianity.

In this climate of no absolutes—except for the rigidly adhered-to belief that there were no absolutes—everything else became possible. It only remained to decide who had enough power to impose his will on the others. Of course in seminaries, those in power teach the courses. The powerless take them. Unless one was willing to teach oneself in the library stacks during the off-hours, there were simply no alternatives offered. The environment was one of contempt for most, if not all, the beliefs that Anglicans had traditionally held, and held well.

Still, I chose to believe that what I had been taught in seminary was an aberration. "Certainly," I reasoned, "the Episcopal Church at large is not this far off course." To its credit, many laity and clergy remained who were still traditionally Anglican. Yet inwardly I knew that mine was not the only class of prospective priests and leaders to receive this kind of indoctrination. My seminary was not the only seminary which held these basic premises. (In fact, my seminary was considered moderate!) A whole body of clergy had been successively taught in this fashion.

HALFWAY TO NOWHERE

The theological liberalism of the seminary was not the only difficulty for me. Another deeply disturbing fact was that Anglicanism, unlike the other major Churches of the Reformation, was not a confessional body. It had no *Book of Concord*, no *Westminster Confession*. Culture was its glue; the *via media* (the middle road) its hermeneutic. The Creed was but a relative statement of faith. A Church which allowed a Bishop Pike to function with a mere censure after denying the Virgin Birth, the Trinity, and the Resurrection was a Church which was more concerned about compromise than truth. The ordination of women to the priesthood was only the bucket of cold water that woke me up. This Church was not going to maintain its fidelity.

The Elizabethan Settlement still prevailed, whether the matters were political, doctrinal, or moral. Revelation, at least Anglican-style, was culturally determined. As the culture continued to decline, so did Anglicanism's message. Abortion, homosexuality, and inclusive language all determined the content, since the Church had to let the world set the agenda for her. The Anglican ethos was founded on a matter of political correctness in the sixteenth century. For me it became painfully obvious that political correctness remained its dominant feature four hundred years later.

Ultimately I became convinced that the *via media* was, in the words of a friend, a path which was leading me halfway to nowhere. I realized I would need to search elsewhere to find an anchor for my faith. I needed more than a church. I needed *the Church*. I needed a place where the Scriptures were not up for grabs, where miracles were not questioned, and where the Incarnation was believed and proclaimed. The Holy Trinity was "excess baggage" in Bishop Pike's theology, yet I knew it was the substance of life in the Kingdom of God.

OUT ON A LIMB

The time for action had come. By now, I had read, studied, and experienced enough about the Orthodox

Church to know that for me there were no other options. Here could be found the organic and historic expression of Christ's Church as it existed unchanged throughout the centuries. It clearly represented all of those things I found lacking in the instability and flux of my seminary experience. Yet I faced a serious mental hurdle.

As an Episcopalian, I had accepted the so-called "branch theory" of ecclesiology, the belief that the many and divergent sects, divisions, and variant strains of Christianity in its current expression represent branches of one tree, a tree which in its entirety comprises the true Church. Because of this belief, I believed that I, too, was already "catholic" and therefore, somehow, *already* a part of Orthodoxy. In fact, I was not. As much as I hated it, I had to come to grips with that fact. However "orthodox" I thought I was, I was not in the Church. There truly was only one Church: there were no branches.

This point was for me, and I think for many Christians looking at Orthodoxy from other Christian backgrounds, the most difficult to accept. Until received into the Church, I was not fully Orthodox. Until received into the Church, I was still playing mental games, no matter how adept I had become at playing them.

In the end, I realized that it was time to quit playing games, and to put an end to living the contradictions and the theological schizophrenia which Reformation theology and its "invisible Church" theory had engendered within me. Poor ecclesiology had kept me an Episcopalian. Poor ecclesiology allowed me to live with compromise and contradiction. The branch theory I clung to as an explanation for multiplicity and disharmony in the

Church kept me from looking for the true unity of the Faith.

Ultimately, it was ecclesiology in particular, not theology in general, which led me to the Orthodox Church. In joining it, I joined the Body of Christ, the same Body which was not only written about in the Book of Acts but which, in fact, *wrote* the Book of Acts. Once my *ecclesiology* became Orthodox, there was no other path for me to take than to become Orthodox. Once I believed that Christ had a visible Body, not one "by heresies distressed," but rather one which held the Faith of the Apostles, the Faith which had established the universe, I had no alternative but to join it.

I confessed that the Orthodox Church was the ark of salvation, that same salvation which was with Noah at the Flood. At last, the criticisms of the "higher critics" were properly critiqued; the culturally conditioned opinions of late twentieth-century Episcopalians were put in context.

When I was ready to embrace Orthodoxy, my Episcopal bishop cautioned me in a rather condescending manner not to expect a Church full of perfect people. I suspect that he thought this an issue of style, of churchmanship. Yet I was not looking for perfection, but for the fullness of the Faith; I was not looking for churchmanship, but for the Church.

In the years which have passed since that time, I have found the lack of perfection all around me, to be sure; but I have also rejoiced in the grace of God which has preserved the Orthodox from all heresy, all falsehood. Flawed people professing a flawless Faith: this is the greatest testimony to the power of the Holy Spirit in the midst of the Orthodox Church.

Since 1981 I have served as priest in the southern tip of Texas, calling people home, calling souls to Orthodoxy, endeavoring bit by bit to extend, by God's grace, His vineyard. Former Anglicans, and also former Roman Catholics and Pentecostals, have answered this call one by one over the years. Having put my hands to the plow, I have not looked back, in spite of all the human frailty I have encountered.

I can only offer the testimony of one who stopped playing church, of one who found the Church in all her fullness. What I found was not merely a branch, a part of the truth but not the whole truth. What I found was literally what Christ established and promised would be here until He comes again in glory: the Church, whole and holy in spite of her sinful members—members just like me.

For the future, I only want to share my experience with others: to declare without reservation that the Church which Christ founded is the Orthodox Church. It is a declaration which I am only too eager to make wherever I am called upon to make it. As part of a preaching mission sponsored by the Romanian Episcopate in 1992, I have even traveled as far as Romania, to one of the world's oldest Orthodox peoples, to share my witness as one who had searched for a city with foundations, whose Maker and Builder was God.

I harbor no illusions about the challenge of converting Americans in large numbers to Orthodoxy. The forms of Christianity known heretofore have been tried and found wanting by so many that it would seem Christianity itself is rejected. Yet, to paraphrase G. K. Chesterton, it is not that Christianity has been tried and found lacking, but that Orthodox Christianity has not been tried at all. To those souls who would take Christ at His word, I would call out, "Shake off your own excess baggage and enter into the joy of your Lord!"

Father John Reeves is pastor of Saint George Church (OCA) in Pharr-McAllen, Texas. He converted in 1977.

A RELUCTANT JOURNEY

by Franklin Billerbeck

It has been a long journey—sixteen years to be exact. But the completion has come quickly. Standing now in a rented basement, facing west, I am asked the all-important question: "Do you renounce all heresies, ancient and modern?"

"I do!"

Within minutes, with my chrismation completed, I will be united with the fullness of the Faith, in communion with most of the ancient patriarchal sees, and under the jurisdiction of the See of Antioch.

What influences have led me to this momentous event in my life?

My formation for Orthodoxy began at my father's knee. From my father, an Episcopal priest, I learned much of the faith and the realities of parochial and priestly life. Unlike many preachers' kids, I loved and lived for the Church. My greatest joy was worship, my fondest memories liturgical. As I served at the altar from age five on, the sights, sounds, and smells of the Maundy Thursday Watch, Benediction of the Blessed Sacrament, and Solemn Mass became indelibly ingrained in my memory.

More a "Catholic-Anglo" than an Anglo-Catholic, I always believed I was first and foremost a member of the One, Apostolic, and Catholic Church, of which Anglicanism (unlike Protestant denominationalism) was a privileged branch. It was, I believed, merely an unfortunate accident of history that we were not in communion with the Orthodox—it never occurred to me that we disagreed with them about the Faith. I believed that Rome, while a branch of the catholic Church, was in serious error.

In 1975 my father retired and we moved to the Eau Claire, Wisconsin, area where, a year later, I would first be exposed to Orthodoxy.

THE FIRST ENCOUNTER

Glancing at a newspaper stand in Minneapolis just as I was about to visit my first General Convention, I learned the news. "Episcopal Church Ordains Women," read the headline. Though barely sixteen, I knew instantly the implications were staggering. By ordaining women the Episcopal Church in the United States of America (ECUSA) was rejecting her catholic identity and everything that identity stood for. Rejecting "mere Christianity," she embraced "mere denominationalism."

I knew I needed to look at other options, and Orthodoxy was the logical choice. My father, who was fully supportive of my position, took me to Christ Church Episcopal Cathedral in Eau Claire, where an exemplary Orthodox priest, Father Paraschou, celebrated the Liturgy once a month. Father Parry received us very warmly. For a year and a half I attended Orthodox services, almost becoming Orthodox in 1978.

What kept me from joining the Orthodox fold right then and there? Several factors. The first was the negative experience of a trusted friend. Saint Luke's Episcopal

Mission in Altoona, Wisconsin, which we attended when my father was not substituting elsewhere, got a new vicar. A faithful priest, this man had actually left ECUSA and joined the Antiochian Orthodox Archdiocese, only to return later to Anglicanism. From him I heard all sorts of horror stories about Orthodoxy. If this priest could not make it in Orthodoxy, I wondered, how could I?

The second factor was my conviction that I had to be loyal to the Episcopal Church. One does not simply "jump branches" because another branch seems more comfortable. "The Church needs soldiers, crack fighting troops at the battlefront. She does not need deserters!" my father had preached. To desert the Episcopal Church would be to deny everything I stood for. Still adhering to the "branch theory," I stayed, fought for my beliefs, and learned much while my father served as substitute priest in the Dioceses of Eau Claire and Fond du Lac. Yet deep down, almost subconsciously, I had an uneasy feeling.

A GRADUAL EXPOSURE

In 1982 I started pursuing graduate studies in Madison, Wisconsin. My father served as Saint Luke's priest-in-charge. (Later, Saint Luke's would take care of my father and mother when they were ill and dying.) I felt an abiding loyalty to this parish. When I attended the Fort Worth Synod, I had high hopes for The Episcopal Synod of America (ESA)—one of my many Anglican hopes to be dashed.

The Holy Spirit used my final years in Anglicanism as a time of great growth for me. After my father's death, Saint Luke's received a new vicar, Father Rowe. With his permission, I published a newsletter for Saint Luke's. As a deputy, I addressed the Diocesan Convention on the subject of evangelism, preached the same message in four congregations, and helped and coordinated evangelism surveys. I was elected a lay delegate to the 1991 General Convention in Phoenix.

Meanwhile there was a strange dichotomy growing within me. The consecration of Barbara Harris as bishop made me realize Anglicanism was quickly becoming unviable. Our branch was being destroyed from within. We in the ESA seemed unable to stop it, yet we were unwilling to take the logical step of excommunication. With fond memories of Father Parry, I reopened my investigation into Orthodoxy.

I started attending a nearby Orthodox Church whenever possible. It seemed to me "ethnic," little interested in evangelism, and not very outgoing. But I kept attending. Gradually I came to know a few people. Soon I felt "at home" with the Liturgy. There was a theological depth, a liturgical stability and a timeless presence of the Kingdom of Heaven I could not find elsewhere. Western services paled in comparison; I now began to look forward to a Sunday away from Saint Luke's.

At last I could feel at ease knowing everyone believed what they were singing. Both from my liturgical experiences and from reading Orthodox books (by authors such as Bishop Ware, Father Schmemann, Father Meyendorff, et. al.), I grew to love and respect Orthodoxy in a new and deeper way. After a year or so I decided that if Anglicanism became utterly untenable, I could become Orthodox, though I felt that with my ethnic background I would always be something of a foreigner.

What was happening was not by chance. One Sunday someone mentioned a Lenten book fair to be held at Holy Apostles Greek Orthodox Church near Chicago. The guest speaker was to be a former evangelical, fundamentalist type who had become Orthodox. A "fundy" converting to Orthodoxy?! This I had to hear!

This guest speaker was Father Peter Gillquist. He shared with us his vision of converting America to Orthodoxy. At last I saw a way that my commitment to evangelism and my attraction to Orthodoxy could walk hand in hand. Here was a vision to which I could dedicate my life! Orthodoxy no longer seemed like a last-ditch option; instead it was a very viable opportunity.

Father Gillquist had joined the Antiochian Orthodox Archdiocese—the same jurisdiction my former Episcopal priest had left behind. I decided to consider Antioch as an option. A former Episcopal priest who lived nearby, Father Bill Olnhausen, had also joined the Orthodox Church through Antioch. Mysteriously, the Holy Spirit prompted me to reread Olnhausen's editorial from *The Evangelical Catholic* entitled "Ten Years Later." If his analysis was correct, and I now thought it was, Anglicanism was flawed at the core and could never be fully and truly catholic. If he was right, I had to become Orthodox. The final debate had begun.

A TIME OF DEBATE

Having discussed the article with my father until he could no longer answer my questions, I sent Olnhausen's article to a number of "conservative" Anglicans—telling them if Olnhausen was right, I had to become Orthodox. I asked them how the Anglican position could be defended against Olnhausen's argument. Only Bishop Wantland of Eau Claire responded. I was stunned and disheartened by the lack of other responses. Immediately taking up Bishop Wantland's offer to talk, I debated the issues between Wantland and Olnhausen over the next year and a half and did more reading. With abiding love I remember the hours Bishop Wantland and Father Olnhausen spent with me. Both are truly committed to our Lord Jesus Christ.

For me, the core of Olnhausen's argument was simple and unavoidable: The Anglican understanding of the Church is fatally flawed. "For Orthodoxy," he argued, "Church is seen as Eucharist—being part of the one Body of Christ which means sharing the one faith: 'One Lord, One Faith, One Baptism.' Partial agreement is not enough. What Orthodox call the Church, therefore, is composed of those who share the One Bread and thus hold the one Faith 'once delivered,' i.e. the Orthodox."

While Anglicans may pay lipservice to the notions of unity in faith being necessary to share communion, and of viewing Church as Eucharist, they do not *de facto* agree with them. A fact I knew only too well was that the ESA shares communion with many who disagree about the faith—i.e., those who ordain women and practicing homosexuals, bless same-sex marriages, use inclusive language, and question the Virgin Birth and the Resurrection. To share communion with those who do not hold the same faith is to be untrue to the faith and practice of the undivided Church, which excommunicated heretics (e.g., Second Ecumenical Council, Canon 1).

"In Orthodoxy," concluded Father Bill, "the Church cannot be split because she always and everywhere holds the same Faith and shares the same Body. One can, however, as previous heretics did, leave the Church. Thus the Anglican understanding and practice of sharing communion is simply not that of the undivided Church." Personally this was very difficult for me, but it did explain why ESA did not break communion with other Anglicans.

I had now reached a critical point in my journey. I could not desert the Church—but was ECUSA the Church? As the debate raged on, it took its toll. A friend said to me over dinner one night, "Franklin, you have to decide. This is tearing you apart." She was right and I knew it. But one last issue had yet to be resolved.

Anglican Catholicism justified itself by the "branch theory." When Rome broke with Orthodoxy in about 1054, England went with her. With the English Reformation, Anglicanism left Rome. If there is one Church, the question is, who was right in 1054? Many Anglicans answered: the Orthodox. But if this was the case, unless we reunited with Orthodoxy, we were not fully Church. Thus began the so-called "branch theory," the notion that the one Church existed in three different branches, each holding the essentials of the Faith, but not in communion with the others due to history and politics.

The theory was flawed, and not even the other "branches" accepted it! In fact, there was not a common faith among them. Our understanding, for example, of the Trinity and of authority differed. (Anglicans and Roman Catholics accept the *filioque*—the clause in the Nicene Creed which says the Holy Spirit proceeds from the

Father *and the Son;* Orthodox do not. Roman Catholics accept papal infallibility; Anglicans and Orthodox do not.) The logical result of a branch theory is disunity in the faith and disunity in the Eucharist. The undivided Church never accepted such a view. As Father Gillquist said, "Anglicans need to give up the branch theory and go with the trunk theory." The truth is, we had left the unity of the Church and we needed to return home. It was so obvious and clear—but so hard to accept. But the branch theory did not sustain itself. To be true to the Church I had to become Orthodox.

One night, not too long before his death, my father had said to me, "You know, if I were a young man like you, I think I would become Orthodox too."

SETTLING IN

Did this mean I would have to deny my past and claim that my years in Anglicanism had been nothing but a sham? No. Our Lord said: "The one who comes to Me I will by no means cast out." And as an Anglican I had come to Him. Orthodoxy was the fulfillment of my faith, not its denial! Orthodoxy does not judge Anglicanism— that is up to God. Orthodoxy simply claims that she alone has the fullness of the Faith and partakes of the One Body.

Because Anglicans do not share the fullness of the Faith—and hence the Eucharist—with the Orthodox, they are not fully united to the Church. This does not mean they cannot be saved or that the Holy Spirit will not work there. It means that Anglicans need to be reunited with the undivided Church, which is possible if and only if they hold the same Faith. This fact took time to accept, but finally accept it I did. And a mysterious thing happened. My anger at Anglicanism started to fade.

Part of my acceptance of Orthodoxy involved shedding my Western legalistic and categorical way of thinking. Gradually I learned the questions were different in Orthodoxy, partly because there was no Reformation or Enlightenment in the East. Also, the answers were not always so clear-cut —not so often "yes" or "no" as "yes and no." In the East there was a greater dependence on God and less on reason—and a greater realization of God's love and mystery. The inner dynamic was different. I learned that one really must approach Orthodoxy on its own terms and not try to impose one's own categories upon it. This takes time, but it is both possible and worthwhile. In the end, it is liberating.

I was deeply impressed by Father Olnhausen's lack of pressure—"Come when you are ready," he said. By spring of 1991 the time had come. Committed but cautious—for I had not yet seen Orthodoxy on a national scale—I attended the Pastoral Liturgical Institute at Saint Vladimir's Seminary regarding the role of women. Here, I thought, I would meet any "radicals," as well as some of the finest of contemporary Orthodox theologians.

I found no radicals but, to my surprise, did meet many former Anglicans, and other wonderful Orthodox people as well. Standing by the porch of Saint Vladimir's refectory as grace was chanted, I suddenly and mysteriously felt at ease, knowing I was home.

TEARFUL GOODBYES

A timetable was set for my conversion. My Anglican duties were completed in November 1991, and it was time to say goodbye. It was harder than I thought. I did not know if I would have any Anglican friends left. Tearfully I told the new vicar of Saint Luke's, Father Rowe, of my decision. He was understanding and supportive. The next Sunday Bishop Wantland visited Saint Luke's. Following service we were alone in the Church. Standing quietly before the very altar where I had served with my father so many times before, I informed him with tears in my eyes of my decision. He understood and put his arm around my shoulder; as with Father Rowe, we parted friends.

Two weeks later, with snow on the ground and a winter chill in the air, Saint Luke's basement was crowded. It would not be easy, but I descended the stairs with determination. Now an Orthodox catechumen, I was fully prepared to have this congregation, which had been my family for the past seventeen years, never speak to me again. With Father Rowe's blessing, I informed them I was becoming Orthodox. Again with tears, I told them why. We are still friends. Two weeks later, on Christmas Eve, I attended my last Episcopalian service—at Saint Luke's, where two years earlier to the day I had served with my father for the last time before his death.

Now it is Epiphany and I am in another basement—where Saint Nicholas Orthodox Mission of suburban Milwaukee meets. That which I have longed for and desired all my life—to be fully part of the undivided Church—is about to come to pass. With the silent glow of candles and the sweet smell of incense and chrism in the air, it is done. I am sealed with the Holy Spirit and united to the Church. A long journey is ended. A reluctant traveler has come home.

REFLECTIONS

Looking back now, I often ask, "Why did I not do this earlier and save so much pain, so many years of bitter conflict?" Yet the Holy Spirit was at work; and who am I to judge? My years in Anglicanism now seem somehow cloudy and confusing, but they were also full of grace. I am thankful to Anglicanism, for it shaped and molded me, giving me a sense of God's love, of who I was and what the Faith was all about. It gave me a sense of vision, of purpose and of ideals. But my vision and my highest Anglican ideals are, and can only be, fulfilled in Orthodoxy. I would be happy nowhere else.

I've learned and grown. Though I am a member of the mission congregation where I was chrismated, I regularly attend that nearby Orthodox parish—where I now feel "at home" and whose people now seem like a friendly, loving and outgoing family. I've come to a fuller understanding of ethos and community. I've met people from a variety of backgrounds who value their roots and their Orthodox Faith. I've had an opportunity to strengthen my spiritual life. I've experienced the presence of the Kingdom of heaven through the Divine Liturgy and icons in a deeper way than ever before. And I've found a purpose—to grow in faith and to help evangelize America with the fullness of Orthodoxy. I could never go back to where I was before.

Unworthy though I am, I dare to thank God for uniting me, the most wretched sinner, to His Holy and Spotless Bride, the Orthodox Church. Truly, He is good and He loves mankind.

Franklin Billerbeck is a member of Saint Nicholas Orthodox Mission (Antiochian), Mequon, Wisconsin.

EPILOGUE

The authors who lived the stories you have just read came from differing backgrounds. But all were Anglicans, all sought Truth and all found it in the Orthodox Church.

The affinity between Orthodoxy and Anglicanism is not new. The vision shared by Archbishop Tikhon and Bishop Grafton truly was a vision glorious. Indeed, many Anglican ideals and people are holy and noble. Anglo-Catholicism grounded itself in the early Church Fathers, seeking nothing more than the "Faith once delivered"— without addition or subtraction. Personal devotion to Our Lord Jesus Christ with a strong scriptural basis was the core of Anglican evangelicalism.

As our authors would agree, Orthodoxy fulfills these ideals. But in Orthodoxy they are brought together in genuine synthesis. Orthodoxy does not have factions, each promoting a different ideal; rather the Church as a whole embraces them all. In Orthodoxy there is fullness and unity, a divine mystery which transcends time and culture.

The ultimate Anglican vision was always a return to the undivided Church. Anglicans prided themselves on being not a mere denomination but mere Christians, in total agreement with the undivided Church throughout the ages. In itself Anglicanism was always narrow and acknowledged its own incompleteness. Thus it tried to be the bridge Church and to serve as a catalyst for Christian unity, hoping to bring the three "branches"—Roman Catholicism, Anglicanism, and Orthodoxy—together and thus reconstruct the One Catholic Church.

The One Catholic Church, however, need not and cannot be reconstructed, for it has never disappeared. Rather it must be entered into; for, as our Lord said, "the gates of Hades shall not prevail against it" (Matthew 16:18). The same undivided Church which gave us the Creed of Nicea still exists today. To fulfill Anglican ideals, all one need do is come home. The Faith and life of the Orthodox Church are not foreign or alien. Rather, this is Truth which embraces all times and cultures. The welcome mat is out, the doors are open, and, if you are committed to the Faith, you are truly welcome.

A short list of recommended reading will be found at the end of this book. We encourage you to visit Orthodox churches and participate regularly in Orthodox worship. For to be truly understood, Orthodoxy must be experienced and lived.

Finally, when you feel it is appropriate, get in touch with one of the contact persons mentioned in the closing informational section. They can help provide direction and put you in touch with some former Anglicans who are now Orthodox. Sometimes it is helpful to talk with someone who shares a similar background. Most importantly, however, we encourage you to pray and to seek God's direction. May Our Lord and Savior Jesus Christ bless and guide you on your journey as you seek to do His most holy will.

FOR MORE INFORMATION ABOUT ORTHODOXY

(Suppliers listed alphabetically within section)

BOOK PUBLISHERS

CONCILIAR PRESS
P.O. Box 76
Ben Lomond, CA 95005
Phone: (408) 336-5118 or (800) 967-7377
(Books, booklets, *AGAIN* Magazine, and brochures. Distributors for the *Orthodox Study Bible*, published by Thomas Nelson, Inc.)

HOLY CROSS ORTHODOX PRESS
50 Goddard Avenue
Brookline, MA 02146
Phone: (617) 232-4544
(Books.)

LIGHT AND LIFE PUBLISHING COMPANY
4818 Park Glen Road
Minneapolis, MN 55416
Phone: (612) 925-3888
(Books, booklets, and brochures, as well as a very complete mail order catalog of items from other sources.)

ORTHODOX CHRISTIAN PUBLICATIONS CENTER
P.O. Box 588
Wayne, NJ 07474-0588
Phone: (201) 694-5782
(Books and brochures.)

SAINT TIKHON'S BOOKSTORE
P.O. Box 1A
South Canaan, PA 18459
Phone: (717) 937-4390
(Books, icons, musical recordings.)

SAINT VLADIMIR'S SEMINARY PRESS
575 Scarsdale Road
Crestwood, NY 10707-1699
Phone: (914) 961-2203
(Books, icons, musical recordings.)

MAGAZINES

AGAIN
P.O. Box 76
Ben Lomond, CA 95005
Quarterly magazine calling the people of God to return to their roots in historic Orthodoxy once again. $12 per year.

THE ANGLICAN/ORTHODOX PILGRIM
P.O. Box 114
Mequon, WI 53092
Quarterly, free-will donation.

THE CHURCH MESSENGER
312 Garfield St.
Johnstown, PA 15906
Published bi-weekly by the American Carpatho-Russian Orthodox Greek Catholic Diocese of the U.S.A. $10.00 per year.

DOXA
Monastery of the Glorious Ascension
P.O. Box 397
Resaca, GA 30735
Quarterly. News, commentary, and current issues. Donation requested to cover cost.

THE ORTHODOX CHURCH
P.O. Box 675
Route 25A
Syosset, NY 11791
OCA monthly newspaper. $10 per year.

THE ORTHODOX OBSERVER
8 East 79th St.
New York, NY 10021
Published bi-weekly by the Greek Orthodox Archdiocese of North and South America. $15.00 per year.

THE PATH OF ORTHODOXY
P.O. Box 36
Leetsdale, PA 15056
Official monthly publication of the Serbian Orthodox Church in the
U.S. and Canada. $10.00 per year.

THE WORD
358 Mountain Road
Englewood, NJ 07631
Official publication of the Antiochian Archdiocese. Published monthly
except July and August. $15 per year.

CORRESPONDENCE STUDY COURSES

Correspondence Department,
Saint Athanasius Academy of Orthodox Theology
Very Rev. Jack Sparks, Dean
9540-2 Central Avenue
Ben Lomond, CA 95005
Phone: (408) 336-9310

The Saint Stephen's Course of Studies
358 Mountain Road
Englewood, NJ 07631
Phone: (201) 871-1355

RECOMMENDED BASIC READING

An Introduction to Western Rite Orthodoxy, Fr. Michael Trigg, editor. The
Western Rite liturgy is a viable option. Includes testimonies of former
Anglican clergy now at home in the Western Rite. (Conciliar Press)

Apostolic Fathers, ed. Fr. Jack N. Sparks. The earliest post-New Testament Christian writings. (Light and Life Press)

Becoming Orthodox, by Fr. Peter Gillquist. The story of 2,000 Protestant
Evangelicals who became Orthodox. Easy to read, sound theology, a
gripping story. (Conciliar Press)

Coming Home, ed. Fr. Peter Gillquist. Personal accounts of eighteen
Protestant clergymen who have journeyed to the Orthodox Faith.
(Conciliar Press)

For the Life of the World, by Fr. Alexander Schmemann. The sacramental life of the Church. (Saint Vladimir's Seminary Press)

Introducing the Orthodox Church: Its Faith and Life, by Fr. Anthony Coniaris. An easy-to-read overview. (Light and Life Press)

The Orthodox Church, by Timothy Ware (Bishop Kallistos). This is the classic introduction to Orthodoxy, written by a former Anglican. (Penguin)

The Orthodox Way, by Timothy Ware (Bishop Kallistos). A superb companion volume to *The Orthodox Church.* (Saint Vladimir's Seminary Press)

CONTACTS

The Rev. Joseph Fester
Director of Evangelism, Orthodox Church in America
404 Tyler Street
Desloge, MO 63601
Phone: (314) 431-4284

The Very Rev. Peter E. Gillquist
Director of Missions and Evangelism,
Antiochian Orthodox Christian Archdiocese of North America
6884 Pasado Road
Santa Barbara, CA 93117
Phone: (805) 968-4014

Fr. Michael Keiser
Dean, Western Rite Vicariate
33736 E. Lake Joanna Dr.
Eustis, FL 32726

His Grace, Bishop MAXIMOS
Greek Orthodox Diocese of Pittsburgh
5201 Ellsworth Ave.
Pittsburgh, PA 15232

Fr. Bill Olnhausen
Anglican/Orthodox Pilgrim
1235 W. Baldwin Court
Mequon, WI 53092

A WORD ABOUT THE FRONT COVER

This book is about journeys to Orthodoxy. Journey involves change. The front cover represents the beginning of the journey (Anglicanism), and is designed to appeal to the Anglican ethos by using a western symbol. However, it should be noted that Orthodox do not use the visual symbol of the lamb to represent Christ. Due to fear of weakening or distorting our understanding of the Incarnation (e.g., giving an impression that Christ's humanity or maleness is not important), Canon 82 of the Sixth Ecumenical Council prohibits the use of the lamb: "Thou shalt not paint a lamb for the type of Christ, but Himself" (Ancient Epitome of Canon LXXXII). In order to safeguard the truth of the Incarnation, Orthodox traditionally have represented Christ through the use of icons. The iconoclasts would accept a lamb figure, but not an icon of Christ.

Icons play a key role in Orthodox spiritual life: they are part of Tradition (the first icon was of the Virgin Mary holding Jesus and was painted by Saint Luke); they help teach and safeguard doctrine; they help reveal God to man and provide us a window into the spiritual realm. Orthodox icons reflect not the views of the painter, but the mind of the Church. They point not to this fallen world, but to the Kingdom of God (hence figures do not look as they would in this world). While at first icons may take some getting used to, the use of Orthodox icons greatly enhances one's spiritual life—as our authors attest. Whereas the front cover represents the beginning of the journey (Anglicanism), the icon below represents the completion of the journey to Orthodoxy.